مصطلحات قانونية باللغة
الإنجليزية

مصطلحات قانونية باللغة الإنجليزية

الدكتور

محمد نصر محمد

أستاذ مساعد القانون بكلية الحقوق جامعة طيبة المدينة المنورة

الطبعة الأولى

1436 هـ/2015 م

مكتبة

القانون والاقتصاد

الرياض

ح مكتبة القانون والاقتصاد، 1435 هـ

فهرسة مكتبة الملك فهد الوطنية أثناء النشر

القطري، محمد نصر

مصطلحات قانونية باللغة الانجليزية ./ محمد نصر القطري .-

الرياض، 1435 هـ

.. ص ؛ .. سم

ردمك: 5-41-8146-603-978

1 - القانون - مصطلحات أ. العنوان

ديوي 340.03 1435/6244

رقم الإيداع: 1435/6244

ردمك: 5-41-8146-603-978

الطبعة الأولى

1436 هـ/2015 م

ISBN 978-603-8146-41-5

مكتبة القانون والاقتصاد
الرياض

المملكة العربية السعودية - الرياض - العليا - ص.ب 9996 - الرياض 11423

هاتف: 4623956 - 2791158 - فاكس: 2791154 - جوال: 0505269008

www.yafoz.com.sa

info@yafoz.com.sa

بسم الله الرحمن الرحيم

Preface

This book has been specially written for beginners in studying English legal terms. Its purpose is to teach law-students how to understand legal material written in English language.

In this book we shall deal with English legal terms in various areas of law, including:

هذا الكتابِ كُتِبَ خصيصاً للمبتدئين في دِراسَة المصطلحات القانونية الإنجليزيةِ. غرضه تعلّيمَ طلابَ القانونِ كَيفَ يَفْهمونَ مادّةَ قانونيةَ كَتبتْ باللغةِ الإنجليزية.

في هذا الكتابِ نحن سَنَتعاملُ مع المصطلحات القانونية الإنجليزيةِ في الموضوعات المُخْتَلِفةِ مِنْ القانونِ، وتَتَضْمن:

Part One: Introduction to Law مقدمات في القانون

Part Two: The Civil Law القانون المدنى

Part Three: The Constitutional Law القانون الدستورى

Part Four: The Criminal Law القانون الجنائى

Part Five: The Public International Law القانون الدولي العام

Part Six: The International Organizations المنظمات الدولية

Part One

Introduction to Law

مقدمة في القانون

Lesson One: General Definition of Law	تعريف عام للقانون
Lesson Two:The Relation Betwee Law & Morality	العلاقة بين القانون والأخلاق
Lesson Three: Divisions of Law	أقسام القانون
Lesson Four: The Legislation	التشريع

Lesson One

General Definition of Law

تعريف عام للقانون

Definition of Law

تعريف القانون

We can define "Law" as the set of obligatory rules which govern and organize the relations in a society.

نحن يُمْكِنُا أَنْ نُعرّفَ «القانونَ» بأنة مجموعة القواعدِ الإلزاميةِ التي تَحْكمُ وتُنظّمُ العلاقاتَ في المجتمع.

Function of Law

وظيفة القانون

Law aims at establishing the order in the society;

we can not imagine existence of a civilized society without existence of the law. The law realizes this aim by determining and protecting of the rights of every individual in the society.

القانون يَهدفُ إلي تنظيم المجتمعِ؛ نحن لا نَستطيعُ تَخَيُّل وجود ِ مجتمع متحضر بدون وجودِ القانونِ. يُدركُ القانونُ هذا الهدفِ بتَقْرير وحِماية حقوقِ كُلّ فرد في المجتمع.

Characters of The Legal Rule

خصائص القواعد القانونية

The legal rules have three characters:

القاعدة القانونية لها ثلاثة خصائص:

A) They are rules governing and conducting the social behavior in the society.

أنها قواعد تنظم سلوك الاشخاص في المجتمع.

b) They are general and abstract rules.

أنها قواعد عامة ومجردة.

C) They are sanctioned by the public authority.

أنها ملزمة بجزاء يوقع بواسطة السلطة العامة.

Exercise

- What are the characters of the legal rules?

--.

Translate into English:

القاعدة القانونية:

كلية الحقوق:

طلاب القانون:

السلطة العامة:

جزاء:

الدين:

الأخلاق:

العرف:

القتل العمد:

Choose the correct answer:

1- The Science which determines and explains the legal rules is:

a) The Science of Law.

b) The Science of Medicine.

C) The Science of Agriculture.

2- The legal rule contains a sanction which can be applied by

a) Law-students.

B) The power of the public authority.

C) Every individual in the society

3- The legal rule which determines the powers of the Dean of College of Law is an abstract rule

A) Because it concerns with one person (the Dean).

b) Because it deals with the Dean by his name.

C) Because it is applicable to all persons who would be candidates for the position of the Dean.

Lesson Two

The Relation Between Law and Morality

The order in the society is mainly based on morality and law. Both of them conduct the behaviour. We can imagine the relation between law and morality as follows:

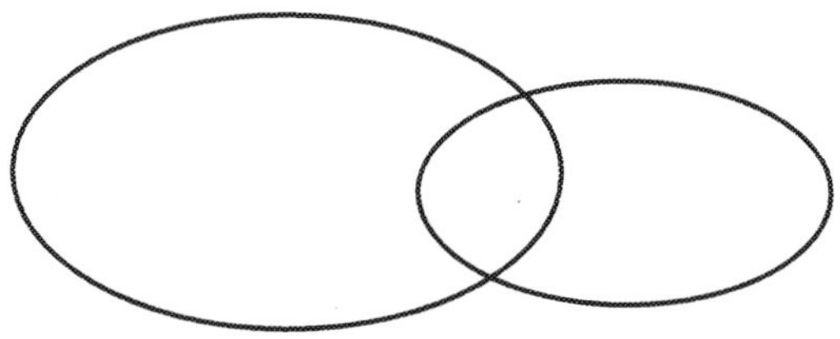

A) indicates the area which morality organizes.

B) indicates the area which law organizes.

C) indicates the interfering area which morality and law organize.

A- Morality:

Morality contains all principles which are considered by the society as obligatory principles which everyone has to respect and follow. If one does not respect moral principle, people in the society will condemn his action.

There is an area which morality organizes and law does not interfere; like the moral rule which asks us to pay charity to poor people and the moral rule which asks us to respect our teachers. Morality contains all the individual's duties and obligations towards the others; so the scope of morality is wider than law.

B- Law:

On the other hand, law contains the obligatory rules which everyone must follow. If an individual does not follow the law, he will be punished by a sanction imposed by the public authority.

There is an area which law organizes alone; like the legal rule which permits drinking alcohol although the morality condemns that.

C) The interfering area between morality and law

There is an interfering area in which morality and law conduct the behaviour in the society; this is because most of the legal rules are derived from morality. Thus the crimes which are punished by the Penal Code are condemned by morality. Also the Civil Code considers the contract which is in contradiction with good morality and public order null[1].

---

(1) See article 2052/ of The UAE Civil Code (UAE Federal Law No. 5 for 1985).

Vocabulary

base.

indicate.

the interfering area.

(A)

principle

consider

moral

condemn

action

pay

charity

poor

duty

obligation

scope

wide

narrow

1985).

(B)

impose

permit

(C)

derive

crime

the Penal Code

the civil Code

contract

contradiction

good morality

public order

null

Exercise

Translate into English:

واجب:

التزام:

جريمة:

التقنين المدنى:

قانون العقوبات:

النظام العام:

باطل:

Choose the correct answer:

1- The scope of morality is

a) narrower than law.

b) equal to the scope of law.

C) wider than law.

2- If one does not respect moral principle,

A) people in the society will condemn his action.

B) he must be punished by a materiel sanction.

C) he must be punished by a sanction imposed by the public authority.

3- The UAE civil code considers the contract which is in contradiction with good morality and public order

a) null.

B) valid.

C) legal.

Lesson Three

Divisions of Law

The law is divided into two divisions:

The Public Law and The Private Law.

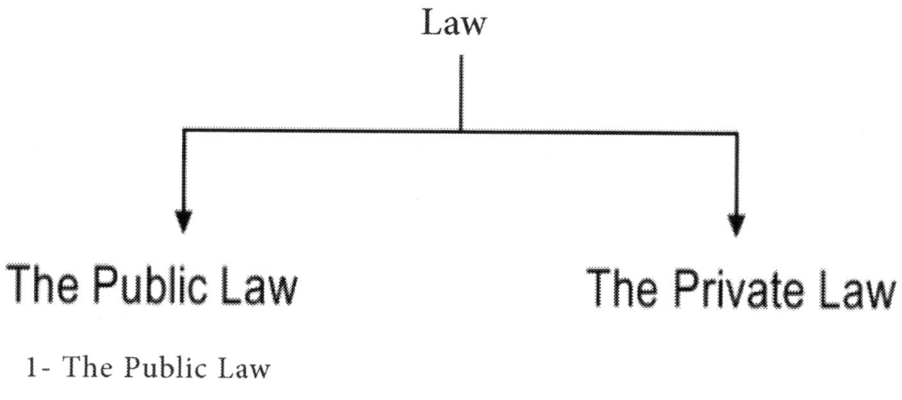

1- The Public Law

The Public Law regulates the relations of public organs (public persons) among themselves and the relations which arise between the individuals and the state or any public organ provided that the state or the public organ acts as a representative of the public authority.

The Public Law gives the state and its public organs certain powers and privileges vis-à-vis the individuals; this is because the public law deals with public interests.

2- The Private Law.

The Private Law regulates the relations which arise between the individuals. The Private Law aims at realizing personal interests.

Example: The contract

- If a contract concludes between two individuals, then it will be a question relating to the private law.
- But if a contract concludes between an individual and the state, so it will be a question relating to the public law.

3- Branches of Public Law.

The main branches of public law are:

- the Constitutional Law.
- the Administrative Law.
- the Criminal Law.
- the Financial Law.
- the Public International Law.

4- Branches of Private Law

The main branches of private law are:

- the Civil Law.

- the Commercial Law.

- the Civil and Commercial Procedure;

- the Private International Law.

Vocabulary

division

divide

The Public Law

The Private Law

(1)

regulate

arise

state

public organ

provided that

representative

power

privileges

vis-à-vis

interests

(2)

personal interest

conclude

(3)

branch

the Constitutional Law

the Administrative Law

the Criminal Law

the Financial Law

the Public International Law

(4)

the Civil Law

the Commercial Law

the Civil and Commercial Procedure

the Private International Law

Exercise

1- What are the main branches of public law?

--.

2- What are the main branches of private law?

--.

Translate into English:

القانون العام:

القانون الخاص:

امتيازات:

العقد:

القانون الدستورى:

القانون الإدارى:

القانون الجنائى:

القانون المالى:

القانون الدولى العام:

القانون المدنى:

القانون التِجارى:

قانون الإجراءات المدنية والتِجارية:

القانون الدولى الخاص:

Choose the correct answer:

1- If a contract concludes between two individuals, then it will be a question relating to

a) the private law.

b) The public law.

c) The criminal law.

2- The main branches of public law are:

a) the Constitutional Law, the Administrative Law, the Criminal Law, the Financial Law and the Public International Law.

B) the Civil Law, the Commercial Law, the Civil and Commercial Procedure and the Private International Law.

C) the Financial Law, the Civil and Commercial Procedure and the Public International Law.

Lesson Four

The Legislation

Legislation is the general rule which emanates from the public authority. It is issued by a public authority; called the legislator or the legislature.

1- Classification of Legislation

Legislation can be classified according to the public authority which issued the legislation. So there are three categories of legislation.

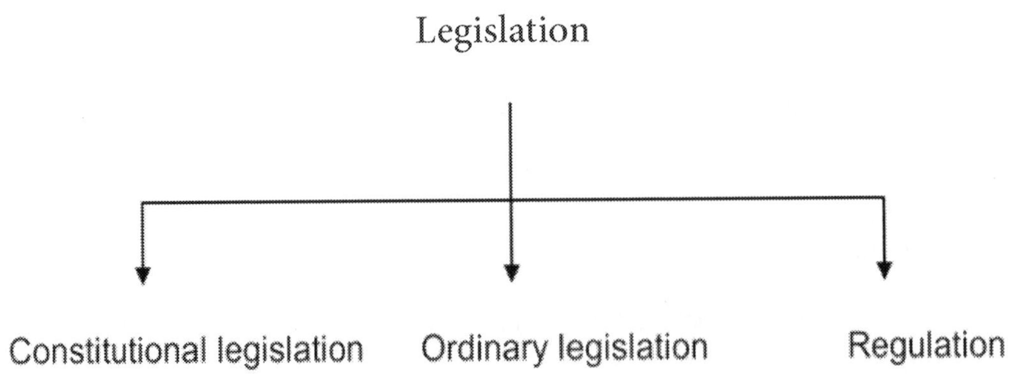

A- The Constitutional legislation (Constitution) emanates from the Constituent Assembly.

B- The Ordinary legislation (Law) emanates from the parliament[(1)].

c- Regulation emanates from the President of the state, ministers and various administrative authorities to which the law delegates this power.

2- The Relation Between the Categories of Legislations

The law can not contravene the constitution and the regulation can not contravene the law. If a law organizes a matter in contrary to the constitution, then the law will be unconstitutional law and also if a regulation organizes a matter in contrary to the law, the regulation will be illegal regulation.

---

(1) According to Article 1102/ of the UAE Constitution, “draft law shall become a law after the adoption of the following procedure:- a. The Council of Ministers shall prepare a bill and submit it to the Union National Assembly.b. The Council of Ministers shall submit the bill to the president of the Union for his approval and presentation to the Supreme Council for ratification. c. The President of the Union shall sign the bill after ratification by the Supreme Council and shall promulgate it. Art. 472/ of the UAE Constitution states “The Supreme Council of the Union shall exercise the following matters: “Sanction of various Union laws before their promulgation, including the Laws of the Annual General Budget and the Final Accounts.” And According to Article 544/ “The President of the Union shall assume the following powers: Signing Union laws, decrees and decisions which the Supreme Council has sanctioned and promulgating them.”

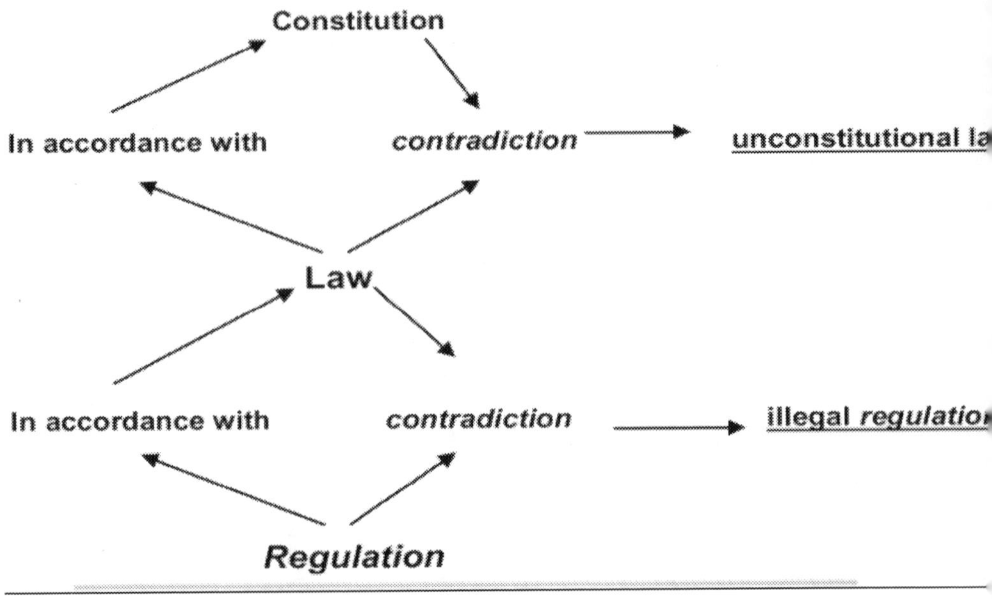

3-The judicial control of the constitutionality of the legislation:

The judicial control of the constitutionality of laws and regulations may be done by the ordinary courts or by a special constitutional court; this depends on the judicial system in the state itself.

In United Arab Emirates, the Union Supreme Court alone undertakes the judicial control in respect of the constitutionality of the laws and regulations. Article 99 of UAE Constitution states "The Union Supreme Court shall have jurisdiction in the following matters:

Examination of the constitutionality of Union laws, if they are challenged by one or more of the Emirates on the grounds of violating the Constitution of the Union.

Examination of the constitutionality of legislations promulgated by one of the Emirates, if they are challenged by one of the Union authorities on the grounds of violation of the Constitution of the Union or of Union laws.

Examination of the constitutionality of laws, legislations and regulations in general, if such request is referred to it by any Court in the country during a pending case before it. The aforesaid Court shall be bound to accept the ruling of the Union Supreme Court rendered in this connection[1].

And according to Article 101 of the Constitution "If the Court, in ruling on the constitutionality of laws, legislations and regulations, decides that a Union legislation is inconsistent with the Union Constitution, or that local legislations or regulations under consideration contain provisions which are inconsistent with the Union Constitution or with a Union law, the authority concerned in the Union or in the Emirate, accordingly, shall be obliged to hasten to take the necessary measures to remove or rectify the constitutional inconsistency.

(1) Article 993 & 2/ of UAE Constitution.

Vocabulary

emanate

issue

the legislator

legislature

(1)

classification

classify

category

constitutional

constitution

the Constituent Assembly

ordinary

People's Assembly

President of the state

Minister

administrative authorities

delegate

(2)

contravene

in contrary to

unconstitutional

illegal

regulation

(3)

the judicial control

constitutionality

the ordinary courts

special constitutional court

the judicial system

The Union Supreme Court

jurisdiction

examination

the Union authorities violation

refer to

pending case

inconsistent with

the necessary measures

Exercise

- Write about the judicial control of the constitutionality of the legislation.

Translate into English:

المشرع:

التشريع الدستورى:

الدستور:

اللائحة:

غير دستورى:

غير قانونى:

المحكمة الاتحادية العليا:

Choose the correct answer:

1- The Ordinary legislation (Law) emanates from

A) the Constituent Assembly.

b) the Parliament.

c) ministers and various administrative authorities.

2- If a law organizes a matter in contrary to the constitution, then the law will be

a) unconstitutional law.

b) constitutional law.

c) legal act.

3- If a regulation organizes a matter in contrary to the law, the regulation will be

A) legal regulation.

B) unconstitutional regulation.

C) illegal regulation.

4- In UAE, the judicial control of the constitutionality of laws is done by

A) the court of first instance.

B) the court of appeal.

C) the Union Supreme Court.

Part Two

The Civil Law

Lesson Five: The Formal Sources of the Civil Law.

Lesson Six: Definition & Classification of The Right.

Lesson Seven: Subjects of Rights (Persons).

Lesson Five

The Formal Sources of The Civil Law

According to the first article of the Civil Transactions Law[1] of the United Arab Emirates, Legislative provisions apply to all matters which are in letter and in spirit organized by these provisions.

In absence of any applicable legislative provision the judge will rule in accordance with the Sharia Islamia[2].

In absence of the Sharia Islamia, the judge will rule in accordance with the custom.

Therefore if the judge does not find any applicable legislative provision then he will rule in accordance with the Sharia Islamia (the Islamic Law) and if he does not find a legislative provision or a solution in the Islamic Law, the judge will resort to the custom.

(1) The UAE Civil Code (UAE Federal Law No. 5 for 1985).

(2) The main sources of the Sharia Islamia are: 1- The Qur'an 2- The Sunnah 3- Ijma' (consensus) 4- Qiyas (analogy).

Thus, the formal sources of UAE Civil Law are:

1- Legislation.

2- Sharia Islamia.

3- Custom.

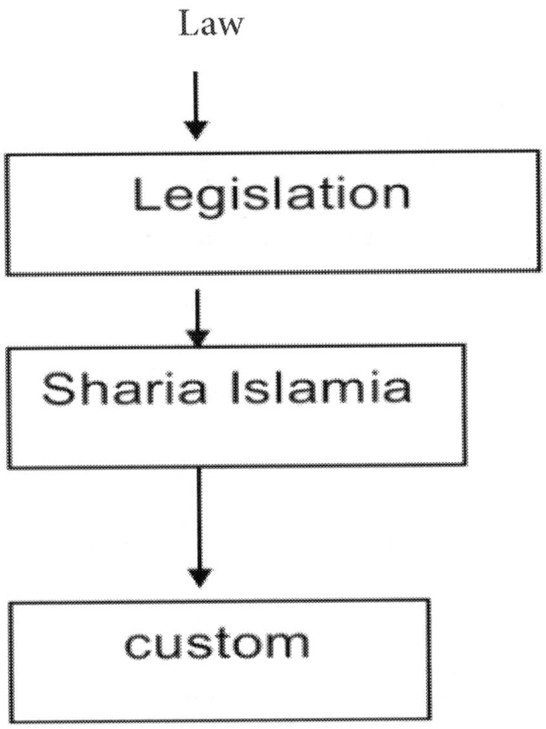

Vocabulary

formal

source

article

legislation

Sharia Islamia (the Islamic Law)

legislative

provision

absence

applicable

in accordance with

resort

custom

judge

Exercise

- What are the formal sources of the UAE Civil Law?

---------------------------.

Translate into English:

التشريع:

قاض:

نص تشريعى:

قاعدة عرفية:

Choose the correct answer

-In UAE, if the judge does not find any applicable legislative provision, he will rule in accordance with

A-The custom.

B- The Sharia Islamia.

C-The rules of natural Law and equity.

Lesson Six

Definition and Classification

of The Right

1- Definition of the right:

The right is an interest protected by the law. This interest may be material or moral. The law confers the holder of the right the powers to secure the enjoyment of his right. Some examples of rights are the right of property and the copyright.

2- Classification of the rights:

Rights can be classified into two kinds; political rights and civil rights.

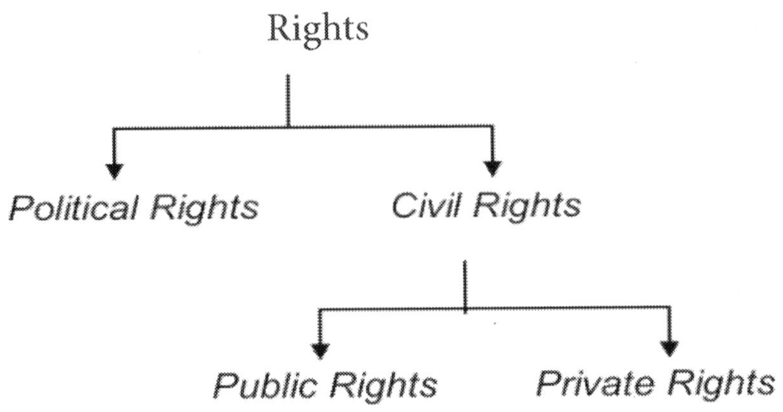

3- Political rights:

Political rights are powers entitling their holder to participate in the government and administration of his country; like the right to vote in the national elections and the right to hold public offices. These rights are not enjoyed by all persons but only by citizens, so, in principle, foreigners are not entitled these rights except by a special legal text.

4- Civil rights:

Unlike the political rights, civil rights are enjoyed by all persons, regardless of their nationalities. The civil rights include individual freedom, the freedom of belief & the freedom of practicing religious rights, the freedom of opinion, the freedom of scientific research, the right to peaceful assembly, the right to form societies, etc.

5- Divisions of civil rights:

Civil rights are divided into two kinds: public rights and private rights.

A- Public rights are necessary for the protection of the personality of the individual. These rights include the right to life, the right of personal security, freedom of conscience, right of honour and reputation, etc.

B- Private rights are enjoyed by particular persons. These rights include family rights, pecuniary rights and incorporeal rights.

Vocabulary

(1)

definition

right

interest

law

material

moral

confer

holder

power

secure

enjoyment

right of property

copyright

(2)

classification

political rights

civil rights

(3)

entitle

participate

government

administration

right to vote

elections

citizen

foreigner

(4)

nationality

individual freedom

freedom of belief

freedom of opinion

freedom of scientific research

right to peaceful assembly

right to form societies

(5)

public rights

private rights

personality

individual

right to life

right of personal security

freedom of conscience

right of honour

reputation

family rights

pecuniary rights

incorporeal rights

Exercise

- Define the right and give some examples of rights?

---.

Translate into English:

القانون:

الحق:

مصلحة :

حق الملكية:

حق المؤلف:

الانتخابات:

المواطن:

الأجنبى:

الحرية الفردية:

حرية المعتقد:

حرية الرأى:

حرية البحث العلمى:

حرية الاجتماع السلمى:

حرية تكوين الجمعيات:

الحق فى الحياة:

الحق فى الحرية الشخصية:

حرية الضمير:

السمعة:

حقوق الأسرة:

الحقوق المالية:

Choose the correct answer:

1- Political rights are enjoyed by

A- all persons.

B- Citizens.

C- Foreigners.

2- All persons, regardless of their nationalities, enjoy

A- political rights.

B- Civil rights.

C- Political rights and civil rights.

Put (√) for true or (X) for false for the following statements

- Rights can be classified into two kinds; political rights and civil rights.

- Civil rights are powers entitling their holder to participate in the government and administration of his country.

- All persons enjoy civil rights.

- Public rights are necessary for the protection of the personality.

Lesson Seven

Subjects of Rights (Persons)

1- The legal personality

The existence of the right demands the existence of a holder of this right. The holders of the rights are persons.

The legal personality is a quality to hold a right and to be bound by a duty. Now every person has a legal personality but in the past slaves were regarded as things so they did not have the legal personality.

2- Kinds of Persons:

Persons are the subjects of rights. There are two kinds of persons: the natural person and the juristic or juridical person (artificial person).

Persons (subjects of rights)

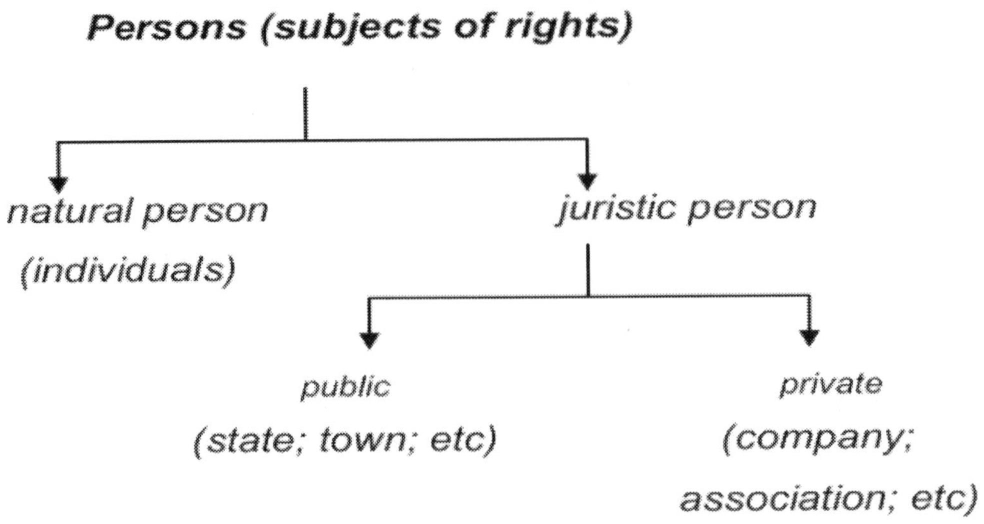

3- The Natural Person:

The natural person is the individual. The legal personality of the natural person begins with his/her birth and ends with his/her death. Although the child conceived is not a real person, the law usually gives him/her certain rights; like the right of succession (if the child is born alive).

A number of legal features distinguish every person from the others; like the name; the domicile; the status; the nationality and the capacity. These features have some legal effects.

The name: Every person has a name distinguishing him/her from the others.

The domicile: The place where the person habitually

resides is his/her domicile. Sometimes, the person has more than one domicile and sometimes he/she does not have any one; like homeless.

The family status: Family status is the position of the person in relation to the other members of his/her family; like single, married, divorced, son, father, etc.

The Nationality: Nationality is the legal relationship between a citizen and his/her state. Such relationship creates certain rights and duties upon the citizens and at the same time the state exercises its diplomatic protection to protect its citizens and their interests. Aliens do not enjoy these rights.

The capacity: Capacity includes the ability of acquiring rights (Capacity of acquiring) and exercising these rights (Capacity of exercise). Every person has the capacity of acquiring regardless of his/her age and he has the full capacity of exercise when he comes of age (in UAE, 21 years).

4- The Juristic Person (juridical Person):

For practical reasons, law recognizes that some entities are subjects of rights. These artificial entities called the juristic or juridical persons.

The juristic persons can be classified into two kinds: public juristic persons and private juristic persons.

Public juristic persons are the state, the provinces, the towns, the villages and the other public authorities.

Private juristic persons are formed by natural persons to achieve a common purpose. This purpose may be pecuniary goal; like companies and may be a non-pecuniary goal; like religious and educational associations.

Vocabulary

(1)

demand

legal personality

quality

duty

slave

(2)

The natural person

The juristic person (juridical person)

(3)

the child conceived

right of succession

the domicile

the status

the nationality

the capacity

homeless

diplomatic protection

aliens

capacity of acquiring

capacity of exercise

come of age

(4)

company

association

Exercise

Exercise

- What are the two kinds of persons?

---.

Translate into English:

الشخصية القانونية:

الشخص المعنوى:

الموطن:

الأهلية:

- Choose the correct answer:

1-In UAE, coming of age is fixed at the age of

A) 18 years.

B) 20 years.

C) 21 years.

2- The natural persons are

A- the companies.

B-the individuals.

C- The associations.

Put (√) for true or (X) for false for the following statements:

- In the past slaves had the legal personality.

- The juristic persons are the individuals.

- Although the child conceived is not a real person, the law usually gives him/her certain rights.

- Every person has the capacity of acquiring regardless of his/her age.

Model Exam

Model Exam

College of Law University of Sharjah

Legal Studies in English

Answer only one:

1- What are the characters of the legal rules?

----.

2- What are the formal sources of the UAE Civil Law?

--------------------------.

Translate into Arabic (only one):

A- The judicial control of the constitutionality of laws and regulations may be done by the ordinary courts or by a special constitutional court; this depends on the judicial system in the state itself. In The United Arab Emirates, the Union Supreme Court alone undertakes the judicial control in respect of the constitutionality of the laws and regulations.

B- The right is an interest protected by the law. This interest may be material or moral. The law confers the holder of the right the powers to secure the enjoyment of his right. Some examples of rights are the right of property and the copyright.

Translate into English:

العرف، جزاء، التقنين المدنى، جريمة، النظام العام، العقد، القاضى.

Choose the correct answer:

1-The legal rule contains a sanction which can be applied by

A) law-students.

B) the power of the public authority.

C) every individual in the society.

2-The scope of morality is

A) narrower than law.

B)equal to the scope of law.

C)wider than law

3- The UAE civil code considers the contract which is in contradiction with good morality and public order

A) null. B) valid. c) legal.

4- If a contract concludes between two individuals, then it will be a question relating to

A) The private law.

B)The public law.

C)The criminal law.

5- The Ordinary legislation (Law) emanates from

A) the Constituent Assembly.

B) the Parliament.

C) ministers and various administrative authorities.

6- If a law organizes a matter in contrary to the constitution, then the law will be

A) unconstitutional law.

B) constitutional law.

C)Legal act.

7- If a regulation organizes a matter in contrary to the law, the regulation will be

A) legal regulation.

B) unconstitutional regulation.

C) illegal regulation.

8- In UAE, the judicial control of the constitutionality of laws is done by

A) the court of first instance.

B) the court of appeal.

C) the Union Supreme Court.

9- In UAE, if the judge does not find any applicable legislative provision, he will rule in accordance with

A) the custom.

B) the principles of Shari'a Islamia.

C) the rules of natural Law and equity.

10- Political rights are enjoyed by

A) all persons.

B) Citizens.

C) Foreigners.

Lesson Eight

The UAE Constitution

دستور دولة الإمارات العربية المتحدة

* The Constitution of The United Arab of Emirates was proclaimed on 18 July 1971 and came into effect on December 2, 1971.

أعلن دستوردولة الإمارات العربية المتحدة في 18 يوليو/تموزِ 1971، ودَخلَ حيّز التنفيذ في 2 ديسمبر/كانون الأول.1971

* According to the first article of the UAE Constitution, The United Arab of Emirates is a federal union consists of the following seven Emirates: Abu Dhabi – Dubai – Sharjah – Ajman – Umm Al Quwain – Fujairah – Ras Al-Khaimah.

طبقاً للمادة الأولي من الدستور الإماراتى ، الامارات العربية المتحدة دولة إتحادية تتكون من سبع إمارات هي: أبوظبى – دبي- الشارقة – عجمان - أم القيوين - الفجيرة – رأس الخيمة.

æ The Union is a part of the Great Arab Nation, to which it is bound by the ties of religion, language, history.

الاتحاد جزء من الأمة العربية ،ويرتبط بها بروابط الدين واللغة والتاريخ.

æ Islam is the official religion of the Union. The Islamic Shari'ah shall be a main source of legislation in the Union. The official language of the Union is Arabic.

الدين الإسلامى هو الدين الرسمى للإتحاد ، والشريعة الإسلامية مصدر رئيسى للتشريع في الإتحاد. واللغة العربية هي اللغة الرسمية في الإتحاد.

The aims of the Union

أهداف الإتحاد

The aims of the Union are: أهداف الإتحاد هي

æ The maintenance of its independence and sovereignty. The safeguard of its security and stability. The defense against any aggression upon its existence or the existence of its member states.

الحفاظ على الإستقلالِ والسيادة. تحقيق الأمن والأستقرار. الدفاع عن أى عدوان يهدد وجودة أو وجودِ دوله عضو فيه.

æ The protection of the rights and liabilities of the people of the Union.

حماية الحقوق والحريات لأشخاص الإتحاد.

æ The achievement of close co-operation between the Emirates for their common benefit in realizing these aims and in promoting their prosperity and progress in all fields.

التعاونِ بين الإماراتِ لتحقيق منفعتِهم المشتركةِ في إدْراك هذه الأهدافِ لإزدهارِهم وتقدّمِهم في كُلّ المجالات.

æ The provision of a better life for all citizens together with respect by each Emirate for the independence and sovereignty of the other Emirates in their internal affairs within the framework of this Constitution.

تحقيق حياة أفضل لكُلّ المواطنين علي السواء وإحترام كُلّ إمارة للإستقلالِ وسيادةِ الإماراتِ الأخرى بما فيها عدم التدخل في الشؤون الداخلية ضمن إطارِ هذا الدستور.

The Union authorities

سلطات الإتحاد

The Union authorities consist of: سلطات الإتحاد تشمل علي

1. The Supreme Council of the Union. المجلس الأعلي للإتحاد

2. The President of the Union and his Deputy. رئيس الإتحاد ونائبه

3. The Council of Ministers of the Union. مجلس وزراء الإتحاد

4. The federal council National. المجلس الوطنى الإتحادى

5. The Judiciary of the Union. السلطة القضائية للإتحاد

Freedoms, Rights and Public Duties

الحريات، حقوق والواجبات عامّة

æ All persons are equal before the law, without distinction between citizens of the Union in regard to race, nationality, religious belief or social status.

كُلّ الأشخاص متساويين أمام القانونِ، ولا تفرقة بين مواطنى الإتحادِ فيما يتعلق بالجنسَ أو الجنسيةَ أو المعتقد الديني أَو المركزالإجتماعي.

æ Personal liberty is guaranteed to all citizens. No person may be arrested, searched, detained or imprisoned except in accordance with the provisions of law.

الحريَّة الشخصية مضمونة لكُلّ المواطنين. فلايجوز أن يُعتَقلُ أو يفَتَّش أو يَحَجزَ أَو يسَجنَ أى شخص إلا بموجب القانونِ.

æ No person shall be subjected to torture.

لا يجوز تعريض أى شخص للتعذيب.

æ Crimes and punishments shall be defined by the law.

الجرائم والعقوبات بنص القانون «لا جريمة ولا عقوبة إلا بنص القانون».

æ Penalty is personal.

العقوبة شخصية (مبدأ شخصية العقوبة)

æ An accused shall be presumed innocent until proved guilty in a legal and fair trial.

المتهم برئ حتى تثبت إدانته.

æ Freedom of movement and residence shall be guaranteed to citizens within the limits of law.

حرية التنقل والسكنى مكفولة للمواطنين في إطار القانون.

æ Freedom of opinion and expressing it verbally, in writing or by other means of expression shall be guaranteed within the limits of law.

حرية الرأى والتعبير شفاهة أوكتابة أو بأى وسيلة من الوسائلة مكفولة في إطار القانون.

æ Freedom of communication by post, telegraph or other means of communication and the secrecy thereof shall be guaranteed in accordance with law.

حرية الإتصال بالبريد، البرق أو وسائل الاتصالات الأخرى وكذلك السرية مكفولة بموجب القانون.

æ Freedom to exercise religious worship shall be guaranteed in accordance with established customs, provided that it does not conflict with public policy or violate public morals.

حرية مُمَارَسَة العبادةِ الدينيةِ سَتُضْمَنُ بموجب العاداتَ، بشرط أن لايحدث تعارض مع السياسةِ العامّةِ (النظام العام) أَو تنتهكُ الأخلاقَ العامةَ.

æ Freedom of assembly and establishing associations shall be guaranteed within the limits of law.

حرية الإجتماع وتكوين الجمعيات مكفولة في إطار القانون.

æ Every citizen shall be free to choose his occupation, trade or profession within the limits of law. Due consideration being given to regulations organizing some of such professions and trades. No person may be subjected to forced labor except in exceptional circumstances provided for by the law and in return for compensation.

كُلّ مواطن ُ حرَّ في إخْتيارَ صناعتة أو تجارتِه أَو مهنتِه ضمن حدودِ القانونِ. ويجب أن يحترم ويطبق التعليماتِ التي تُنظّمُ مثل هذه المِهَنِ والتجارةِ. ولا يجوز إخضاع أى شخصَ قسراً إلى العملِ الإجباري ماعدا في الظروفِ الإستثنائية.

æ No person may be enslaved.

لا يجوز اسعباد أى شخص.

æ Every person shall have the right to submit complaints to the competent authorities, including the judicial authorities. Concerning the abuse or infringement of the rights and freedoms.

كُلّ شخص له الحقّ فى تَقديم الشكاوى إلى السلطاتِ المختصة ، بما فيها السلطاتِ القضائيةِ. بشرط عدم إساءه الإستخدام أَو إنتهاكِ الحقوقِ والحريات.

æ Payment of taxes and public charges determined by law is a duty of every citizen.

دفع الضرائب والرسوم العامة بموجب القانون واجب علي كل مواطن.

æ Defense of the Union is a sacred duty of every citizen and military service is an honor for citizens which shall be regulated by law.

الدفاع عن الإتحاد واجب مقدس على كل مواطن ، والخدمة العسكرية شرف للمواطنين بموجب القانون.

æ Respect of the Constitution, laws and orders issued by public authorities and public order and respect of public morality are duties incumbent upon all inhabitants of the Union.

إحترام الدستورِ والقوانينِ والقرارات الصادرة عن الإدارات العامّةِ والنظام العامِ وإحترامِ المبادىء الأخلاقيةِ العامّةِ واجب على كُلّ سكان الإتحادِ.

Vocabulary

The Constitution

Article

The UAE Constitution

Religion

Language

Common destiny

Maintenance

Independence

Sovereignty

Safeguard

Security

Stability

Defense

Aggression

Existence

Achievement

Close co-operation

Common benefit

Citizen

Internal affairs

The foreign policy

Consolidation

Friendship

The Supreme Council of the Union

The President of the Union

Deputy

The Council of Ministers

The National Assembly

The Judiciary

Freedom

Public duties

Equal

Distinction

Race

Nationality

Religious belief

Social status

Personal liberty

Arrest

Search

Detain

Imprison

Torture

Degrading treatment

Crime

Punishment

Penalty

The accused

Innocent

Guilty

A legal and fair trial

The case

Freedom of movement

Residence

Freedom of opinion

Freedom of communication

Worship

Custom

Public policy

Violate

Public morals

Freedom of assembly

Forced labor

Compensation

Complaint

The competent authorities

The judicial authorities

Taxes

Military service

Honor

Public authorities

Public morality

Inhabitants

Exercise

What are the aims of the Emirates Union?

---.

Write about the foreign policy of the Emirates Union (according to the Constitution)?

---.

What are the authorities of the Emirates Union?

--.

Write about freedoms, rights and public duties in the UAE Constitution.

------.

Translate into English:

السيادة:

الأمن:

الاستقرار:

الشئون الداخلية:

السياسة الخارجية:

المجلس الأعلى للاتحاد:

رئيس الاتحاد:

مجلس الوزراء:

المجلس الوطنى:

القضاء:

الواجبات العامة:

الجنسية:

الحرية الشخصية:

التعذيب:

جريمة:

عقوبة:

المتهم:

برئ:

مذنب:

حرية التنقل:

حرية الرأى:

حرية المراسلات:

حرية الاجتماع:

الأخلاق العامة:

تعويض:

ضرائب:

Put (√) for true or (X) for false for the following statements:

1 - All persons are equal before the law.

2 - No person may be arrested, searched, detained or imprisoned except in accordance with the provisions of law.

3 - No person shall be subjected to torture.

4 - Crimes and punishments can be defined by the bylaws.

5 - No penalty can be imposed for any act of commission or omission committed after the relevant law has been promulgated.

6 - The accused is presumed guilty until proved innocent in a legal and fair trial.

7 - No person may be enslaved.

lesson nine

definition of the criminal law

تعريف القانون الجنائي

the criminal law is mainly concerned with prevention and punishment of the crime. it divides into two main branches:

يهتم القانون الجنائي بشكل رئيسي بالمنع وعقار الجريمة وينقسم إلى فرعين رئيسيين

A) penal law: قانون العقوبات

B) law of criminal procedures قانون الإجراءات الجنائية

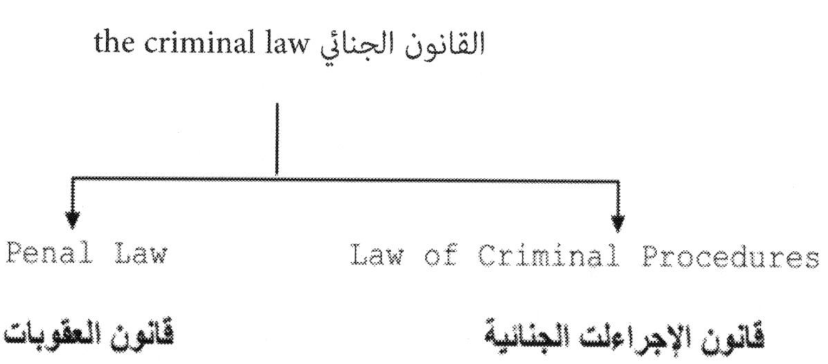

A) penal law

قانون العقوبات

- the penal law contains the provisions which determine the crimes and its penalties.

قانون العقوبات يحتوي على المواد التي تفرز الجرائم وعقوباتها

B) law of criminal procedures

قانون الإجراءات الجنائية

- the law of criminal procedures contains the provisions which organize the method which must be followed to investigate, prosecute and punish the guilty persons.

قانون الإجراءات الجنائية تحتوي على المواد التي تنظم الطرق التي يجب أن تتبع في التحقيق والمحاكمة ومعاقبة الأشخاص المذنبين

Vocabulary

the criminal law

prevention

punishment

crime

penal law

law of criminal procedures

penalty

investigate

prove

violation

prosecute

punish

guilty

Exercise

- what are the main branches of the criminal law?

----

translate into English:

قانون العقوبات

قانون الإجراءات الجنائية:

عقوبة:

مذنب:

choose the correct answer:

- the criminal law divides into two main branches:

A) law of treaties and law of the sea.

B) penal law and law of criminal procedures.

C) space law and diplomatic law.

Lesson Ten

Elements of the Crime

أركان الجريمة

The term "crime" means a positive or negative act threatens the order and security of the society and this act is regarded as a legal wrong which can be punishable.

مصطلح جريمة يقصد به كل فعل خطأ إيجابي أو سلبي يهدد النظام وأمن المجتمع وهذا الفعل المخالف للقانون يكون عرضة للعقاب.

The crime has two elements required to establish the criminal responsibility. These two elements are the material element and the mental element.

للجريمة ركنان أساسيان لقيام المسؤوليةِ الجنائية هذان االركنان هما الركنَ الماديَ والركن المعنوى.

- The material element consists of an illegal act, prohibited criminal result and causation between the illegal act and the result.

الركن المادي يَشْملُ كل فعلٍ غير مشروع ، وعلاقة سببية بين هذا الفعل والنتيجة .

- The mental element requires the existence of the mental intention.

الركن المعنوى ويقصد به القصد الجنائى

Vocabulary

Threaten

Order

Security

Criminal responsibility

Material element

Mental element

Exercise

What are the elements of crime?

--------------.

Translate into English:

المسئولية الجنائية:

القصد الجنائى:

ركن مادى:

ركن معنوى:

Lesson Eleven

Classifications of crimes

تقسيمات الجرائم

1- Classifications of crimes as to the nature of the wrong

تقسيمات الجرائم بالنظر إلي طبيعة الخطأ

A) Crimes threaten the security of the state(the political crimes):

These crimes include all offences against security, peace and property of the state.

الجرائمُ التى تهدد أمنَ الدولةِ (الجرائم السياسية):

تَتضمّنُ هذه الجرائمِ كُلّ المخالفات ضدّ الأمنِ والسلامِ وملكيةِ الدولةِ.

Examples of these crimes are: corruption and its related crimes, as spy and terrorism.

أمثلة هذه الجرائمِ: الفساد والجرائم ذات العلاقة، كالجاسوسية والإرهاب.

B) Crimes against the rights of the individual:

جرائم الاعتداء على حقوق الأفراد

These crimes include all offences against private interest which are divided into crimes against persons (e.g. homicide and battery) and crimes against property (e.g. theft and breach of trust).

تَتضمّنُ هذه الجرائمِ المخالفة أو الاعتداء على المصلحة الخاصةِ، وتنقسم هذه الجرائمِ إلى جرائم الاعتداء على الأشخاصِ (ومثال على ذلك: القتل والضرب) وجرائم الاعتداء على الملكيةِ (ومثال على ذلك: - سرقة وخيانة أمانة) .

2- Classification of crimes as to its structure

تقسيمات الجرائم وفقاً لبناءها

A) Simple crimes: These crimes consist of a single illegal act. Examples of these crimes are: murder, rape and battery.

جرائم بسيطة: هذه الجرائمِ تَشْمل فعل غير شرعي وحيد أمثلة هذه الجرائمِ: القتل وإغتصاب والضرب .

B) Compound crimes: These crimes consist of several compound illegal acts; such as robbery which includes theft coupled with violence.

جرائم مركّبة: هذه الجرائمِ تَشْملُ عِدّة أَفْعال غير شرعية مركّبة؛ مثل السرقةِ المقترنة بعنفَ أو اكراه.

C) Habitual crimes: These crimes include several illegal acts which are considered as one crime, such as prostitution.

الجرائم الإعتياد: تَتضمّنُ هذه الجرائمِ عِدّة أَفْعال غير شرعية وتعتبرجريمة واحدة، مثل الدعارةِ.

D) Continuous crimes: These crimes include illegal acts which are happened through a continuous and uninterrupted length of time.

Examples of these crimes are: possession of unlicensed weapons and possession of stolen property.

الجرائم المستمرة: تَتضمّنُ هذه الجرائمِ أَفْعالَ غير شرعيةَ التي حدثت وتستمر طول مستمر فترة من الزمن . أمثلة هذه الجرائمِ : إمتلاك الأسلحةِ غير مرخصة وإمتلاكِ المواد المسروقةِ.

3- Other classifications of crimes

تقسيمات أخرى للجرائم

Also, crimes can be classified to many kinds; like:

- positive crimes & negative crimes.

- Complete crimes & incomplete crimes.

- Ordinary crimes, economic crimes, political crimes, military crimes, etc..

أيضاً، جرائم يُمْكِنُ أَنْ تُصنّفَ إلى العديد مِنْ الأنواعِ؛ مثل:

* جرائم إيجابية وجرائم سلبية.

* جرائم كاملة وجرائم ناقصة.

* جرائم عادية، جرائم إقتصادية، جرائم سياسية، جرائم عسكرية، الخ

In UAE, according to the Federal Penal Law, Crimes are divided into:

- Hudood crimes,

- Crimes of Qisas and Diyya;

- Tazir crimes.

في الإمارات العربية المتحدة، طبقاً لقانونِ العقوبات الإتحادي،

الجرائم منقسمة إلى:

1- جرائم الحدود ،

2- جرائم الدية والقصاص ؛

3 - جرائم التعزير.

Crimes are classified to three kinds: felonies; misdemeanors and contraventions.

الجرائم تُصنّفُ إلى ثلاثة أنواعِ: الجنايات ؛ الجنحة والمخالفات

- The felony is the crime which is punishable by one of the following penalties:

والجنايات كجريمة يعاقب عليها بالعقوبات الأتية :

1- Penalties of Hudood or Qisas.عقوبات الحدود والقصاص

2- Capital punishment (death penalty); عقوبة الأعدام

3- Permanently imprisonment (life imprisonment); السجن المؤبد

4- Temporary imprisonment. السجن المؤقت

- The misdemeanor is the crime which is punishable by one or more of the following penalties:

جرائم يعاقب عليها بعقوبة أو العقوبات الاتية:

1- Detention (confinement); الحجز أو الجبس

2- The fine; الغرامة

3- The Diyya. الدية

4- Whipping (flogging) in Hudood of drinking alcohol and defamation.

الجلد لشرب الخمر أو تشويه السمعة أو الإساء إليها.

The contravention is every act which is punishable in laws or regulations by the following two penalties or by one of them:

المخالفات: وهي كل فعل يعاقب عليه القانون بالعقوبتين الآتيتين أوإحداهما:

1- Detention for a period not less than 24 hours and not more than 10 days.

الحبس مده لا تقل عن 24 ساعة ولا تزيد عن 10أيام.

2- The fine which is not more than one thousand dirhams.

الغرامة التى لا تزيد عن ألف درهم.

Vocabulary

Threaten

Order

Security

Criminal responsibility

Material element

Mental element

causation

mental intention

Nature

Wrong

Political crimes

Offences

Property

Controversial

Corruption

Spy

Terrorism

Private

Crimes against persons

Homicide

Battery

Crimes against property

Theft

Breach of trust

Structure

Simple crimes

Illegal

Act

Murder

Rape

Battery

Compound crimes

Robbery

Violence

Habitual crimes

Prostitutions

Continuous crimes

Uninterrupted

Possession

Unlicensed

Weapons

Stolen property

The Federal Penal Law

Hudood crimes

Crimes of Qisas and Diyya;

Tazir crimes

Felonies

Misdemeanors

Contraventions

Penalty

The fine

Compensation

Punishable

Drinking alcohol

Defamation

Capital punishment (death penalty)

Permanently imprisonment (life imprisonment);

Temporary imprisonment

Detention (confinement)

Whipping (flogging)

Exercise

What are the elements of crime?

--------------.

- Classify crimes according to its structure?

----------------------.

- What do we mean by «simple crimes»?

--------------.

Translate into English:

المسئولية الجنائية:

القصد الجنائى:

الجريمة السياسية:

الرِشوة (الفساد):

الإرهاب:

جرائم ضد الأشخاص:

القتل:

الضرب:

سرقة:

خيانة أمانة:

الاغتصاب:

السطو:

الدعارة:

أسلحة غير مرخصة:

جناية:

جنحة:

مخالفة:

الإعدام:

السَجن مدى الحياة:

الحبس:

الغرامة:

Choose the correct answer:

- According to The UAE Penal Code, felonies are the crimes which are punishable by the following penalties:

A) Any penalty from penalties of Hudood or Qisas except Hudood of drinking alcohol and defamation; Capital punishment (death penalty); Permanently imprisonment (life imprisonment) and Temporary imprisonment.

B) Detention or/and fine which its maximum level exceeds one hundred dirhams.

C) Fine which is not more than one hundred dirhams.

Lesson Tweleve

Divisions of Law

تقسيمات القانون

the law is divided into two divisions: ينقسم القانون إلى قسمين

the public law and the private law. القانون العام والقانون الخاص

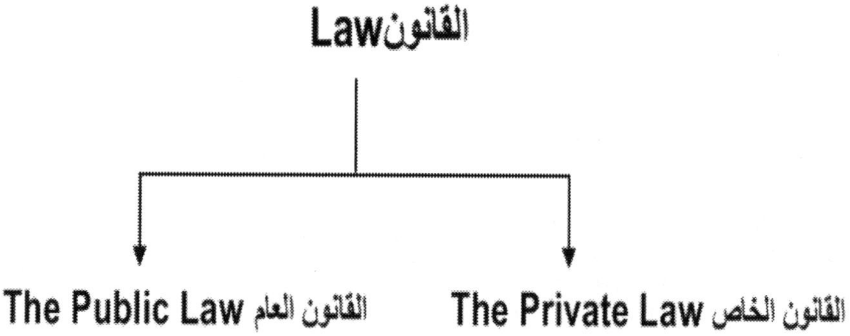

1- The Public Law: القانون العام

the public law regulates the relations of public organs (public persons) among themselves and the relations which arise between the individuals and the state or any public organ provided that the state or the public organ acts as a representative of the public authority.

ينظم القانون العام العلاقات فيما بين الأشخاص العامة وكذلك العلاقات بين الأفراد أو الأشخاص العامة والدولة بشرط أن الدولة أو الشخص العام ينصرف كممثل للسلطة العامة.

the public law gives the state and its public organs certain powers and privileges vis-à-vis the individuals; this is because the pubic law deals with public interests.

يعطي القانون العام الدولة والأشخاص العامة بعض السلطات والامتيازات بالقياس إلى الأفراد، لأن القانون العام يتعامل مع المصالح العامة.

The public law gives the state and its public organs certain powers and privileges vis-à-vis the individuals; this is because the public deals with public interests.

يعطي القانون العام الدولة والأشخاص العامة بعض السلطات والامتيازات بالقياس إلى الأفراد؛ لأن القانون العام يتعامل مع المصالح العامة.

2- the private law: القانون الخاص

the private law regulates the relations which arise between the individuals. the private law aims at realizing personal interests.

ينظم القانون الخاص العلاقات بين الأفراد فالقانون الخاص يستهدف تنظيم المصالح الشخصية.

3- branches of public law: فروع القانون العام

The main branches of public law are	فروع القانون العام هي:
The constitutional law;	القانون الدستوري
The administrative law;	القانون الإداري
The criminal law;	القانون الجنائي
The financial	القانون المالي
The public international law.	القانون الدولي العام

4- Branches of private law: فروع القانون الخاص

The main branches of private law are	فروع القانون الخاص هي:
The civil law;	القانون المدني
The commercial law	القانون التجاري
The civil and commercial procedure;	قانون الإجراءات المدنية التجارية
The private international law;	القانون الدولي الخاص

Vocabulary

division

divide

the public law

the private law

regulate

arise

state

public organ

provided that

representative

power

privileges

vis-à-vis

interests

personal interest

conclude

branch

the constitutional law

the administrative law

the criminal law

the financial law

the public international law

the civil law

the commercial law

the civil and commercial procedure

the private international law

Exercise

1- what are the main branches of public law?

2- what are the main branches of private law?

----

translate into English

القانون العام:

القانون الخاص:

امتيازات:

العقد:

القانون الدستوري:

القانون الإداري:

القانون الجنائي:

القانون المالي:

القانون الدولي العام:

القانون المدني:

القانون التجاري:

قانون الإجراءات المدنية والتجارية:

القانون الدولي الخاص:

Choose the correct answer

1- if a contract concludes between two individuals, then it will be a question relating to

A) the private law.

B) the public law.

C) the criminal law.

2- the main branches of public law are;

A) the constitutional law, the administrative law, the criminal law, the financial law and the, public international law.

B) the civil law, the commercial law, the civil and commercial procedure and the private international law.

C) the financial law, the civil and commercial procedure and the public international law.

Table of Contents

Supject	Page
Preface	7
Part One: Introduction to Law	9
Lesson One: General Definition of Law	11
Lesson Two: The Relation Between Law and Morality	15
Lesson Three: Divisions of Law	21
Lesson Four: The Legislation	28
Part Two: The Civil Law	37
Lesson Five: The Formal Sources of the Civil Law	39
Lesson Six: Definition & Classification of The Righ	43
Lesson seven: Subjects of Rights (Persons)	53
Model Exam	61
Lesson eight: The UAE Constitution	65
Lesson nine: definition of the criminal law	81
Lesson Ten: Elements of the Crime	85
Lesson Eleven: Classifications of crimes	89
Lesson Twelve: Divisions of Law	103
Table of Contents	111

Legal Studies in

English

Legal Studies in English

Prepared By

DR.MOHAMED NASSR

College of law

First copy

1436 / 2015

Law & Economy Bookshop

Riyadh

مكتبة
القانون والاقتصاد
الرياض

Printed in the United States
By Bookmasters